This Question Notebook

If found, please return to: _____

_____
_____
_____
_____

Just Curious: A Notebook of Questions

JUST CURIOUS

A NOTEBOOK OF QUESTIONS

by Kendall Long

I dedicate this book of questions to my incredible parents,
Bob and Michele, who have always taken the time to feed my curiosity for
the world around me.

CONTENTS

10   Introduction:
      Why, You Ask?

16   Always Ask Why:
      Got Questions?

318   Conclusion:
      Reflections

Why write a book full of questions? Because *I wanted answers*—but not just any answers; I wanted answers that could show me who we truly are. As the old saying goes: *"It is not the answer that enlightens, but the question." – Eugene Ionesco*

    I am extremely curious by nature and spend many of my days enthralled by the happenings of everyday life, in both our urban and natural worlds. I've traveled all over the place, meeting countless people above and below the equator, hopping from country to country over vast expanses of water and interacting with countless different shades of life; but incredibly, the more people I meet, the more that I realize how difficult it is to actually get to know someone.

    Often, the nature of my connections seemed to me somehow trivial. How could I hold a conversation for hours and still end up miles from understanding someone? Most of our lives revolve around small talk: we exchange pleasantries with supermarket cashiers and acquaintances we see at the dog park; we ask coworkers "how are you?" perhaps without listening to their answers; and slowly we lose access to each others' inner worlds.

    The more aware of this I become, the more active I am in making an effort to understand the people I encounter. How can I see each individual in a new light, one that my prior conversations failed to enrich? What little trick was I missing? The answer came to me one night after going on a first date. At this point in my life, I was freshly single and enjoying many first dates, thanks to the simple convenience of dating apps. Searching within a certain square mileage to obtain my dream partner was right at my fingertips and tempted me with

Introduction
WHY, YOU ASK?

its mysterious allure on most weekends. During this time of exploration, somehow all of my first dates seemed monotonous or overly uniform. We always exchanged the same kinds of stories, aspirations, and questions.

It wasn't that I didn't want to know things, like where they were born, how many siblings they had, or where they'd gone to school; I just got tired of answering all those same questions myself! On more than one occasion, I would mistakenly forget to whom I'd told what and be met with a sigh of familiarity as I retold the same scripted dialogue from my past. It was almost as if I were presenting a slideshow entitled **The Spark Notes of Kendall Long.** There was no meat to these stories, only bullet points scratching the surface of who I really am. I know first dates are traditionally a place to cover the basics, but I didn't want to be basic. What good did this vetting process do for either one of us, if we were only looking at the surface most level of attraction? I needed to expedite dating in this new world of opportunities. I needed different questions.

My curiosity drove me to write down new questions and expand upon the **getting to know you** process. I would jot them down every time I dreamt them up! I started collecting questions from everywhere and everyone. Never knowing when inspiration would hit, I made it a habit to carry around a small notebook with me at all times. Nuzzled between an aged leather wallet and whatever book I might have been reading at the time, there would be my question book, ready and waiting for me to jot down a query at any moment's notice. But these couldn't be just any questions. They needed to be questions that could unravel the defensive nature of human beings, springing a leak in the mundane lull of everyday conversation. After years of jotting them down, I had accumulated quite a collection (a few hundred, in fact)! In time, an entire book arose, filled to the brim with questions and doodles, which became insightful snapshots of the growth I'd experienced on my journey into authenticity and connection.

I tested out a few questions on dates and experienced tremendous enrichment in my conversations. Inspired, I introduced these questions at social gatherings and discovered the same effect. My relationships were not only improving—they were becoming richer and more accessible. This is when I learned about the strength of the vulnerability of connection; so much so that I almost became addicted to prying back the layers of my innermost torments to display them to my peers. Remarkably, they did the same. Openness with one's self inspires openness in others, and this is what connection is all about. I have grown so much from this collection of questions; and now, some years later, I find myself wanting to share the power of these questions with this big beautiful world.

In this book, I have put together 150 of my absolute favorite questions, here for you to carry in your quest for deeper connection. The first step in this quest is to become curious about the stories hidden in the people around us. The more inquisitive and curious we become, the deeper the connections we forge and the more that we love. Love doesn't have to be romantic; it doesn't even have to be reciprocated. I think love is just the admiration of knowing and understanding someone for who they really are—to see a glimpse of complete

Introduction: Why, You Ask?

vulnerability and connect with all that makes us so beautifully ourselves. We experience less fear when we get to know each other, and our hearts open in new ways. We see parts of ourselves outside the context of **ourselves**; and this, for me, is the true nature of love. Love is about discovering ourselves in other people.

From our commonality for error to the music we dance to and the food that fuels our bodies, why does it matter how different or alike we might feel? We relate by just that: relating! Often we're more alike than we care to admit, but upon taking the time to truly understand someone, a candle flares in the spirited corners of our minds. We feel all that was missing from the shadows, as words are illuminated on the pages of others' stories, bringing to light all that has been forgotten or unacknowledged. This book is more than a list of words printed on paper: it is a gateway to real human connection. The dimensions we have yet to discover in each other go far beyond the everyday, even amongst our closest friends and family members!

One personal example of this goes back to a perfect summer day, not too long ago, when I was lazing by the pool with my sister. I'm closer with my sister than I am with most people in the world, and I attribute this to our being identical twins. We have spent most of our lives together, learning from our experiences side by side. While we basked in the sun on our lounge chairs that day, I brought out my question notebook to pass the time. Of course, at first I expected to know most of her answers, however I was amazed to find that my knowledge of her fell short! We only got through about three to four questions (our conversation took the scenic route and sprouted many tangents), but on that day, I gained perspectives on her inner life that I didn't have before. Sitting in the sun, I saw my identical twin (the mirror image of myself), as something completely different. It was a great experience, enough to make me believe in magic again.

So, start filling in these pages. Bring this book to life in your own, unique way. Be inquisitive and bring this book to parties, school, family reunions, first dates (maybe even on your 100th date) and especially on your travels. Anytime an opportunity presents itself, whip out this book and ask someone a question! Ask the person sitting beside you on the bus; ask your teacher, mother, or perhaps even your new crush—literally, ask everyone you meet! You will be surprised by their answers and graced with new understanding about who they really are, as their hearts open to yours.

There is only one rule for using this book: never let an answer rest in yes or no. Always go further and ask "Why?" **Why** is literally my favorite word of all time, for it holds the key to knowledge, adventure, and finding our way back home. **Why** is a humble word with just three letters; but when used correctly, it offers us so much more. When is the correct time to use this infamous word, you might ask? **All** of the time! **Why?** Because it represents all that we don't yet know but yearn to understand in time. Among the five W's, "Why" is certainly the secret password for cutting-edge wisdom and knowledge.

Introduction: Why, You Ask?

To start us off, I will ask the first question: Are you fearless and vulnerable enough to show people your true self? Regardless of the question, do you solemnly swear to answer back to the world with why?

Always Ask Why
GOT QUESTIONS?

QUESTION 1   What is your favorite smell?

QUESTION 2

You have the ability to grant one person one wish:

Who gets the wish?

QUESTION 3

What is the most common reason that people come to you for help?

QUESTION 4

Let's say magic is real:

What spell do you learn first?

QUESTION 5

What is the best compliment you ever remember receiving?

QUESTION 6

What first impression do you normally make on new people?

QUESTION 7   What is the last photo you took?

QUESTION 8

What advice can you give me about life (or love, loss, happiness, sadness)?

QUESTION 9

If you were reincarnated as a famous landmark, which landmark would it be?

QUESTION 10   What is your favorite thing to
                                shop for right now?

QUESTION 11

Would you rather exchange some looks for intelligence, or some intelligence for looks?

QUESTION 12

If humans came with warning labels, what would yours say?

QUESTION 13

What is the most beautiful view you have ever experienced?

QUESTION 14

What is the last book that you read?

QUESTION 15

What phobia or irrational fear do you experience?

QUESTION 16

What's your favorite thing to do on the Internet?

QUESTION 17

What would you do if you found $50 on the ground?

QUESTION 18

Which sense would you choose to eliminate, if given no other choice, or which sense would you choose to enhance?

QUESTION 19

What can you see outside your bedroom window?

QUESTION 20

Do you have any nicknames for people in your life?

QUESTION 21

Among your friends and family, what are you famous for?

QUESTION 22

When was the last time you did something kind for someone?

QUESTION 23

What is something special about where you grew up?

QUESTION 24

What is your earliest memory?

QUESTION 25

What would be the most annoying thing about having yourself as a roommate?

QUESTION 26

What does the most recent text that you sent say?

QUESTION 27

Is there something that you never thought you'd do, until you did it?

QUESTION 28

What is the most depressing meal you have ever eaten?

QUESTION 29

What is the most unusual food you have ever eaten?

QUESTION 30

If you found an alien gun that could blow up one item to 100x its size, what item would you enlarge?

QUESTION 31

What is the most uncomfortable place in which you've ever slept?

QUESTION 32

What purchase represents the best $20 you've ever spent?

QUESTION 33   Do you collect anything?

QUESTION 34

What is your best story from a wedding?

QUESTION 35

Imagine a clock that counts down to one milestone in your life:

To what event would you set the clock?

QUESTION 36

If you could make a thirty-second phone call to yourself at any one point in your life (present or future), when would you call and what would you say?

QUESTION 37

As a child, what is something about adulthood that you expected to be really amazing but actually isn't that amazing?

QUESTION 38

What personal moment would you like to go back and undo?

QUESTION 39

What was cool when you were a kid but isn't cool now?

QUESTION 40

What are the first three things that you remember wanting to become in life?

QUESTION 41

Compare the person you were ten years ago to the person you are today:

Which differences are you happy about and which ones make you sad or nostalgic?

QUESTION 42   What picture do you love the most?

QUESTION 43

Who was your first enemy (or your first best friend)?

QUESTION 44

Would you trade your most cherished memory for the chance to re-experience the moment itself (knowing that it might be different the second time around)?

QUESTION 45

Tell me about three things that frightened you as a child.

QUESTION 46

If you were arrested with no explanation, what might your friends or family assume that you'd done?

QUESTION 47

If you had a giraffe and needed to hide it somewhere, what hiding spot would you choose?

QUESTION 48

As a child, what did you believe for way too long?

QUESTION 49

If you had five-million dollars to spend on opening a small museum, what kind of museum would you create?

QUESTION 50

If you could make one rule for everyone to follow, what would the rule be?

QUESTION 51

Out of all your past birthdays,
which one was your favorite?

QUESTION 52

What advice would you give your child about love?

QUESTION 53

If you were invisible for one day, how would you spend it?

QUESTION 54

If you could convince everyone in the world to do one thing at the same time, what would it be?

QUESTION 55

How do you hope to change as a person in the future?

QUESTION 56

What is the most ridiculous thing you've ever bought?

QUESTION 57

On what topic could you give a 45-minute presentation with absolutely no preparation?

QUESTION 58

If you were a dictator of a small island nation, what crazy dictator stuff would you do?

QUESTION 59

If you were visiting an isolated community where the local tradition was to eat someone who'd passed away, would you try human meat?

QUESTION 60

If you were a ghost and could possess people, what would you have them do?

QUESTION 61

If you were given one thousand acres of land that you didn't have to pay taxes on but couldn't sell, what would you do with it?

QUESTION 62

If you had to sum up the entire human species in three words, what words would you choose?

QUESTION 63

What do you think would happen if tomorrow there were scientifically-verified evidence that aliens exist?

QUESTION 64

If you could obtain one animal body part in place of your own, which one would you replace?

QUESTION 65

Imagine that there's a zombie apocalypse at this very moment:

What is your plan?

QUESTION 66 If you could have an unlimited amount of anything in the world (not including money, gold, diamonds, etc.), what would you want to have?

QUESTION 67

If a song played every time you entered a room, what would it be?

QUESTION 68

If something you drew could come to life, what would you draw?

QUESTION 69

If you could live anywhere in the world for one year, where would you live?

QUESTION 70

Do you have a good relationship with your neighbors?

QUESTION 71

At what age did you learn the most about yourself?

QUESTION 72

When was the last time you told someone that you loved them?

QUESTION 73

When was the first time that someone broke your trust?

QUESTION 74

What do you not regret that you probably *should* regret?

QUESTION 75

What are three things you keep in the freezer at all times?

QUESTION 76

What about the opposite sex confuses you the most?

QUESTION 77

What are the most important rules to follow on a first date?

QUESTION 78

What is the best shared trait between you and your parents?

QUESTION 79

What do you appreciate most about your family?

QUESTION 80

Do you like your name, and would you ever change it?

QUESTION 81

What are some personal "rules" that you would never break?

QUESTION 82   What was your first impression of me?

QUESTION 83 Tell me about your first kiss.

.

QUESTION 84   What is the last lie that you told?

QUESTION 85

Tell me about the first time you tried alcohol.

QUESTION 86

What is your favorite flaw in yourself (or perhaps in someone you love)?

QUESTION 87

If you could pass just one personal attribute onto your children, which one would you choose?

QUESTION 88

What aspect of yourself do you wish more people could see?

QUESTION 89

If you were single, would you kiss the last person that you kissed again?

QUESTION 90

What do you need help with most often?

QUESTION 91

If you had to live one day as a household appliance, which appliance would you choose?

QUESTION 92

What is your least favorite holiday?

QUESTION 93

What are three things that you need in a significant other?

QUESTION 94

In what subject would you want to be an expert?

QUESTION 95

What adventure have you always wanted to go on?

QUESTION 96   What attracts you to someone?

QUESTION 97

What songs have you completely memorized?

QUESTION 98

What is your favorite part about your daily routine?

QUESTION 99

What is the most impressive thing you know how to do?

QUESTION 100

Tell me about a moment in which you realized you were in love.

QUESTION 101

What is the craziest thing that you've ever done in the name of love?

QUESTION 102

What was your first experience with death?

QUESTION 103

If you could know the truth behind every conspiracy but would die instantly if you were to hint at knowing that truth, would you still want to know?

QUESTION 104

What is the most illegal thing
you've ever done?

QUESTION 105

What do you fear that people will see when they look at you?

QUESTION 106

What would a mirror opposite of yourself be like?

QUESTION 107

Which of your scars has the best story behind it?

QUESTION 108   When is the last time you cried?

QUESTION 109

When is the last time you yelled at someone?

QUESTION 110

What is the worst piece of advice you have ever received?

QUESTION III

Have you ever had a life-threatening experience?

QUESTION 112

If there was a non-returning voyage to colonize the moon, would you want to go?

QUESTION 113　　What is good about death?

QUESTION 114

Do you believe humans are born inherently good or evil?

QUESTION 115

When was the last time that you were mean to someone?

QUESTION 116

If you had to choose between living for five years on Mars, or in the deepest part of the ocean, which would you choose?

QUESTION 117

Tell me about a time when you felt really scared.

QUESTION 118

What frightens you most about yourself?

QUESTION 119

What are you most afraid of losing?

QUESTION 120

What are some things that you've needed to unlearn?

QUESTION 121   Have you ever stolen anything?

QUESTION 122

Tell me about the last time you genuinely connected with someone.

QUESTION 123

What would you like to have happen to your body after you die?

QUESTION 124

If you were to disappear and start a whole new life, how would your new life look?

QUESTION 125

Where do you see the world in 100 years?

QUESTION 126

What was the last thing you chose to let go?

QUESTION 127

What would be your first question upon waking up from being cryogenically frozen for 100 years?

QUESTION 128

What question would you like to have answered about the universe?

QUESTION 129

What's the hardest lesson that you've had to learn?

QUESTION 130

What lesson took you the longest to learn?

QUESTION 131

What would a world populated by clones of you be like?

QUESTION 132

If you had the ability to enhance one characteristic of the human population, what characteristic would you choose?

QUESTION 133

When was the last time that you experienced awe?

QUESTION 134

Would you want to know the whole truth about something, even if it made life harder for you?

QUESTION 135

What is the weirdest thing about modern life that most people accept as normal?

QUESTION 136

How would you react if there were irrefutable proof that God exists?

QUESTION 137

Where do you think consciousness goes when we die?

QUESTION 138

What role does spirituality play in your life?

QUESTION 139

A genie offers you one wish that expires tonight:

What do you wish for?

QUESTION 140

What is the closest you've come to "Heaven on Earth"?

QUESTION 141

What, if anything, would you actually enjoy about Hell?

QUESTION 142

If you built a theme park, what would be the theme and some of the rides?

QUESTION 143

Would you rather be reincarnated with all of your past memories, or is it better to start over fresh?

QUESTION 144

If you had a video of one event from your childhood, which event would you like to re-watch now?

QUESTION 145

Imagine the world was rewound by one year and everybody lost their memory except for you:

What would you change?

QUESTION 146

Finish this sentence,
"Right now I'm feeling..."

QUESTION 147

What have been the highest and lowest parts of your life?

QUESTION 148

What *physical* attribute do you hope that humans will acquire in one million years?

QUESTION 149

What superpower would you give to all the children in the world?

QUESTION 150

Let's say that the meaning of life on earth is whatever you want it to be:

What higher purpose would you choose for yourself right now?

Now this is not the end. It is not even the beginning of the end. But it is, perhaps, the end of the beginning. - Winston Churchill

In exploring these pages, I hope that you have found discovery. It is my ambition to offer you the gift of curiosity, along with a thoughtful look into the lives of other human beings. This question book serves as a reminder to dive a little deeper and stay fearless in how we approach vulnerability. Scribbled amongst these pages lies the history of your connections with other people; these answers, doodles, and quotes are purely unique to the individuals with whom you have crossed paths, whether these relationships became lifelong friendships or stayed with you for just a short while.

    This collection of questions has deeply impacted the way I see other people in this life. Conversations and relationships have diverged onto paths I never could have anticipated, and I hope you can derive just as much enlightenment from the lives of the people around you as I have, perhaps even more! In times of stress, when the world seems to be dissolving

Conclusion
REFLECTIONS

around us, our connections serve as the true strength and foundation beneath our feet. We all have that mischievous inner dialogue that brings with it our doubts and despairs; but we serve as the heroes for each other in our shared struggles. The gift of humanity lies in learning through each others' battles and triumphs—rising to the challenge of opening ourselves up to others and sharing the stories that make us so wonderfully unique.

And, as always:

be curious

be fearless

ask questions.

KENDALL LONG
Just Curious: A Notebook of Questions

Copyright © 2020 by Kendall Long

First edition

ISBN: 978-1-7356200-0-8

All rights reserved under International and Pan-American Copyright Conventions. Manufactured in the United States of America.

No part of this publication may be reproduced, stored in or introduced into a retrieval system, or transmitted in any form or by any means (electronic, mechanical, photocopying, recording or otherwise) without the prior written permission of the publisher. This book is sold subject to the condition that it shall not, by way of trade or otherwise, be lent, resold, hired out, or otherwise circulated without the publisher's prior written consent in any form of binding, cover, or condition other than that in which it was published.

BOOK DESIGN Stephanie MacDougall
EDITOR Kelsey Straight
PUBLISHING SUPPORT The Self Publishing Agency

Made in the USA
Coppell, TX
21 December 2020